Pigeon

KEEPING
FANTAIL PIGEONS

OTHER TITLES AVAILABLE OR PLANNED

Concise Fancy Pigeon Standards

Racing Homer

West of England Flying Tumbler

Exhibition & Flying Pigeons

Fancy Pigeons & Their Management

Join the ***World Bantam & Poultry Society*** which also represents pigeons. (address as for Beech Publishing House)

KEEPING
FANTAIL PIGEONS

JACOB BARRETT

Beech Publishing House
Spur Publication Books Ltd
7 Station Yard
Elsted Marsh
MIDHURST
West Sussex   GU29 0JT

ISBN 1-85736-213-6

Second Edition 1996
New Impression with Colour Plate
of Fancy Pigeons 1997

A catalogue entry is at the British Library,

Beech Publishing House
Spur Publication Books Ltd
7 Station Yard
Elsted Marsh
MIDHURST
West Sussex   GU29 0JT

CONTENTS

Foreword

Fantails are one of the most attractive of pigeons and are extremely tame when kept in an aviary. Moreover, following the normal rules of aviculture–– suitable accommodation and a correct diet , they will breed and provide endless hours of interest.

This guide is based on the works of others and the first hand experience of the author who keeps and breeds these fascinating birds.

J Barrett

A Silver Fantail

A winner from long ago when Silvers were being established.

COLOUR PLATE

The colour plate opposite shows a variety of Fancy Pigeons, number 6 being the Exhibition Fantail. Note the unique features of the fantail; no other pigeon listed resembles it in any significant manner.

White Fantail Hen
Excellent conformation, but tail rather spoilt ; a top winner in condition.

FANCY PIGEONS

1. Black Mottled Short-faced Tumbler; 2. Red Long-faced Tumbler; 3. Beard Tumbler; 4. Almond Tumbler; 5. Suabian Pigeon; 6. Fantail; 7. Priest; 8. Magpie; 9. Jacobin; 10. Baldhead; 11. Turbit; 12. Barb; 13. Domino; 14. English Owl; 15. Blondinette; 16. Turbitt; 17. Trumpeter; 18; Swallow; 19. White-spot; 20. Dragon; 21. Antwerp; 22. Runt; 23. Carrier; 24. Pouter; 25. Norwich Cropper; 26. Nun; 27. Yellow Spot. 28. Shield; 29. Frill Back; 30. Homer; 31. Archangel; 32. Swift; 33. Modena; 34. Hyacinth (next 22)

CHAPTER 1

EVOLUTION OF THE PIGEON*

ARTIFICIAL SELECTION AND NATURAL SELECTION

The naturalists Charles Darwin and Alfred Russel Wallace drew up a theory of evolution. Darwin in particular gave pigeons as a prime example. I, therefore, propose to follow Darwin, and would warn you against almost inevitable disappointment, for it is with common-place things and facts of every-day occurrence that a great theory has to deal.

ARTIFICIAL SELECTION

DOMESTIC PIGEONS

Darwin early in his enquiry felt the importance of having individual animals and birds under close observation, so that all conditions influencing them could be determined. For this purpose *domestic* animals were far more suitable than wild ones, and pigeons were selected for special study for these reasons:

1. The evidence of their descent from a common ancestor is clear;
2. Their historical records extend back many centuries;
3. Their variations are very great, all kinds being easily kept in captivity and all breeding true.

There are probably more than 250 kinds of pigeons known which breed true,and these differ constantly from each other. A

*Based on a paper prepared by Prof. C.F. Marshall

detailed explanation of these is to be found in *Fancy Pigeon Standards* , issued by the National Pigeon Association.

The chief varieties are the following. (See Fig. 1.1)

The *Pouter* is a large and upright bird with a long body and long legs, a moderate–sized beak, and a very large crop and oesophagus. It has the habit of inflating its crop, producing a "truly astonishing appearance", being then "puffed up with wind and pride".

The *Carrier* is a large bird with a very long beak. The skin round the eyes, over the nostrils, and on the lower jaw is much swollen, forming a prominent wattle.

The *Barb* has a short and broad beak, and a wattle of moderate size.

The *Fantail* has tail feathers to the number of 34 or more ––32 being usual –– twelve being the normal number in a fancy pigeon. **The tail is expanded and held erect. It has a peculiar gait, and a curious habit of trembling by convulsive movements of the neck. In a good specimen the way the pigeon stands should allow the back of the head to touch the tail. Sometimes authors state that:** *the tail should be long enough to touch the head* , but this is incorrect because a garden fantail may have a long tail which does *not* touch the head.

The *Turbit* has a **frill** formed by divergent feathers along the front of the neck and breast. The beak is very short.

The *Tumbler* has a small body and short beak. During flight it has the habit of turning involuntary back somersaults.

The *Jacobin* has long wings and tail and a moderately short beak. It has a **hood** formed by the feathers of the neck.

The *Trumpeter* has a tuft of feathers at the base of the beak, curling forwards. The feet are much feathered. The *coo* is very peculiar, and unlike that of any other pigeon, being rapidly repeated and continued for several minutes.

Among these forms there is thus great diversity in both form and colour. This diversity also affects the internal structure,

Figure 1.1 A Group of Fancy Pigeons

for example the skull: the caudal and sacral vertebrae and also the ribs vary in number. The number of primary wing and tail feathers, the shape and size of the eggs, the manner of flight, and almost all other characters, also differ. If these birds were now found in a wild state, they would be considered to constitute distinct genera, yet they are known to be all descended from *Columba livia*, the Blue Rock Pigeon of Europe, Africa, India, etc.

The arguments brought forward by Darwin to prove this are as follows:–

1. All domestic races are highly social, and none of them habitually build or roost in trees; hence it is in the highest degree probable that their ancestor was a social bird nesting on rocks.

2. Only five or six wild species have these habits, and nearly all these but Columba livia can be ruled out at once.

3. *Columba livia* has a vast range of distribution – from Norway to the Mediterranean, from Madeira to Abyssinia, and from India to Japan. It is very variable in plumage and very easily tamed. It is identical with the ordinary dove–cot pigeon, and except in colour practically identical with toy pigeons generally.

4. There is no trace of domestic pigeons in the feral condition.

5. All races of domestic pigeons are perfectly fertile when crossed, and their mongrel offspring are also fertile. Hybrids between even closely allied species of pigeons are, on the other hand, sterile.

6. All domestic pigeons have a remarkable tendency to revert in minute details of colouring to the Blue Rock Pigeon. This is of a slate–blue colour, with two bars on the wings, and a black bar near the end of the tail. The outer webs of the outer tail-feathers are edged with white: these markings are not seen,

together in any other species of the family.

PROOF BY EXPERIMENT

This tendency to *revert* was demonstrated by Darwin as follows:

He first crossed a white fantail with a black barb; then a black barb with a red spot (a white bird with a red tail and a red spot on the forehead). He then succeeded in crossing the mongrel barb–fantail with the mongrel barb–spot, and the birds produced were blue, with markings on the tail and wings *exactly like those of the ancestral rock–pigeon.* Thus two black barbs, a red spot, and a white fantail, produced as grandchildren birds having every characteristic of *Columba livia,* including markings found in no other wild pigeon.

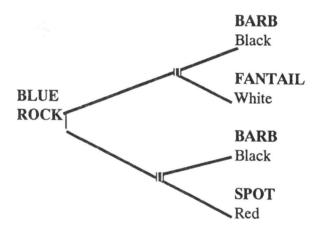

7. All domestic pigeons resemble *Columba livia* in their habits. They all lay two eggs, and require the same time for hatching. They prefer the same food, and *coo* in the same peculiar manner, unlike other wild pigeons.

A Blue Rock Pigeon and a Pouter Pigeon.
**All tame pigeons have evolved from the Blue Rock Pigeon (or Dove); a
comparison with the pouter shows extreme variation ; in fact, the fantail is
not too far removed from the BRP.**
All domesticated pigeons have a common ancestor in the Blue Rock Dove so
in effect these are variations of one species . The many wild pigeons which
exist are not compatible with the domesticated varieties.

6

8.   *Columba livia* has been proved to be capable of domestication in Europe and in India.

9.   *Historical Evidence* – Referring to Aldrovandi, who figured pigeons in the year 1600, we find the Jacobin with a less perfect hood; the Turbit apparently without its frill; the Pouter with shorter legs, and a less remarkable bird in all respects; the Fantail with fewer tail feathers, and a far less singular appearance; the Tumbler existed then, but in none of the short-faced forms; the Carrier had a beak and wattle far less developed than the modern English Carrier. These were the same groups of pigeons, but with their distinctive characters less marked, thus showing convergence towards their common ancestor.

TWO FUNDAMENTAL LAWS

The mode of action of these changes is by *artificial selection*, or the power possessed by man of influencing the shape, size, and colour of animals by the accumulation of small differences in successive generations. This depends on two laws:

1.   *The Law of Variation*, depending on the fact that no two animals are exactly alike.
2.   *The Law of Inheritance*, or the tendency to hand down characters and peculiarities to descendants.

The variation in form occurs from geographical locations and from habits adopted, eg; change of diet. Those birds kept in aviaries can be induced to behave in specific ways to affect the type of offspring bred.In fact, once domesticated, changes which might have taken hundreds of years may be brought about in just a few years.We have only to look at the breeds of fancy pigeons

7

Figure 1.2 Front view of Fantail.
Symmetry is essential , yet with the distinctive on toe stance.

to see how many distinct varieties now exist, many of which are relatively new ,eg; Antwerp Smerle, has been recognized in Britain only since the 1930s.

With the *Inheritance factor* we have to recognize that domestication and breeding to a written *standard* has resulted in greatly exaggerated features being bred into pigeons.Fantails have to have large tails and therefore breeders have paired together birds which excel in tail size and number of feathers as well as having a prominent breast and having a tendency to strut and shake, especially with Exhibition Fantails.

Obviously the *Survival of the Fittest Law* , introduced by Darwin,applies in a restrictive sense with birds being selected for breeding by the bird–keeper and often such stock may suffer from severe limitations . Some pigeons may not even be capable of hatching and rearing their young; in the case of the Exhibition Fantail eggs may have to be given to surrogate mothers, especially early in the season.

8

Figure 1.3
A Picture from the Past : White Fantail being examined.

T. A. W . Deekes a well known breeder 60 years ago.

*Mr Deekes always emphasized the importance of a good, solid,
thick cushion--essential for carrying a srtong tail , the main
feature of the Fantail.   Obviously this should be viewed in
relation to the size of the bird, but must be strong enough to hold
the tail.*

Tail 32 feathers
Medium length
Thickly thatched
ie, double round
of broad feathers

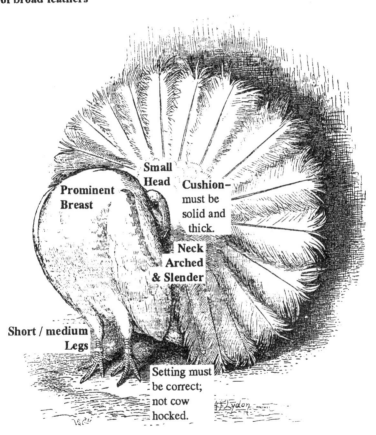

Small
Head

Cushion-
must be
solid and
thick.

Prominent
Breast

Neck
Arched
& Slender

Short / medium
Legs

Setting must
be correct;
not cow
hocked.

Fig.2.1 Basic Features Of Fantail

There should be balance , body action (trembling) , and a symmetrical tail
of an height which is in harmony with the rest.

10

CHAPTER 2
THE FANTAIL DESCRIBED

INTRODUCTION

This graceful bird is undoubtedly the most generally known and admired of the many varieties belonging to fancy pigeons; not only is it held in high esteem by the best of fanciers, but it is eminently popular with the general public. Of this charming and fairy-like bird I would now give a brief outline:

It is a Pigeon of great beauty, and also of great antiquity, all the old writers on Pigeons alluding to the Fantail -- or *Broad-Tailed Shaker* as it was originally called - in most eulogistic terms. Discussions have taken place as to the origin of the Fantail, the consensus of opinion being that it is a native of India. Be this as it may, the fact remains that the Fantail is extensively bred in India and in many countries besides the United Kingdom. Further, it may be assumed that the Fantail can claim a greater number of admirers outside the ranks of professional fanciers than perhaps any other variety of Pigeon. The charming arrangement of the tail, graceful carriage, and vagaries of movement, entitle the Fantail to the high distinction of being considered "the lady's bird"; anyway, ladies (as well as gentlemen) generally bestow a good deal of attention to the Fantail classes at the various Shows. So popular indeed are the "Fans" that a Show, without a class for them, must be likened to the play of Hamlet without the ghost.

ESSENTIAL REQUIREMENTS

There are two leading properties appertaining to the Fantail. One of these is very tangible - the *tail* - the other is wholly feather points, without the accompaniment of constant tremulous motion and high strung action may supply indeed a beautiful sample of Nature's choicest feathered flowers, but to use the language of a well-known votary of the Fantail , such a sample is but "an image", beautiful indeed in its proportions and delineations, but motionless and completely devoid of evidence of that life and style which alone constitute a typical Fantail.

The name "Shaker" is often used to describe it. How much is implied in this name will best be gathered by watching the tip-top, tip-toe Fantail go through its marvellous and graceful performances in a commodious and well-adapted walking-pen, the pedestal on which it exhibits its charms of feather display and graces of bodily action to the gaze of the spell-bound pigeon fancier; for to take all this in one must be not only an admirer of Nature superficially, but rather a devotee of the Fantail itself.

A GENERAL DESCRIPTION

We now proceed to describe the Fantail's physical proportions, and then, secondly, its artistic performances – the former under the heading of **body and feather**, the latter under that of motion and action.

THE BODY – In *size* , this should be rather below that of the ordinary pigeon – a *small body* is, indeed, much esteemed; the *back* and *keel* bones should be rather short, the one very full at the breast and the other wide and slightly raised in structure at the buttock end, thus supplying a basis, both in the front and, at the rear, for a well-displayed , prominent chest and a full, close-feathered rump or "cushion", rising in increasing fullness and without any break from the middle of the back to the ultimate rise of the secondary feathers, which support the tail in a perfectly erect position. On these two fundamental points of structure all the excellences of feather display depend.

Fig 2.2 Tail of Fantail --32 feathers normal

Fig. 2.3 Fantail which does not have the essential stance of the top-class bird.

13

In shape, the body, divested of all plumage, should present, except at the tail–end, rather a **round** than an oval appearance; so it differs diametrically from most others of its kind. A most important part of its physical construction depends on a great projection of the chest, so that, while the length from the front of the breast to the rise of the tail may seem not far less than that of many other varieties, yet the neck being very much thrown back, even to touching the cushion at the base of the tail, gives to the Fantail an appearance, which really is no more than an appearance, of having a short back ; hence in show reports we frequently read of a "good short back"; which really means that the chest is so prominent, and the head and neck thrown so far back towards the tail as to give the beautiful apparent formation of a short spinal bone underlying the feather covering.

Not only should the neck be well thrown back, but it should be arched, lengthy, and slender. The head should be small, narrow, and rather dove–shaped, presenting a somewhat snaky appearance. The eye should, in whites and parti–coloured birds, be of a deep hazel colour, termed frequently "bull–eyed". In blacks and blues, as well as reds and yellows , the iris may be either deep orange or pearl silver. The legs are rather short, but should present a very sprightly and spring–like appearance. They should be free from all feathers below the hocks*; the claws are slender and very flexible.

FEATHER – I prefer a Fantail to be neither exceedingly long nor short in the tail feathers. As a rule, the longer the feather the more "image–like" is the bird, while on the other hand, the very short–feathered specimens have not the tail so well spread, and at times they seem quite incapable of maintaining their balance. A well–proportioned tail goes a long way, not only in exhibiting a good feather display, but also in controlling a

*The exception is the Indian Fantail described later.

graceful performance in action. The **tail** cannot be carried too erect, or be too round, flat, and close in its spreading.

As a rule birds with from thirty–two to thirty–four tail feathers prove the most circular, flat, and well–fitting in tail; such birds are known to have the feathers so evenly touching each other without any break or irregularity as not only to be quite close at the upper part of the circle, but they so nearly join at the extremes at each side as to present an absolutely continuous circle, even at the spot where, being parted, they meet each other at the base.

The **wings** should fit close to the sides at the upper end of the body, sloping gracefully downwards towards the tail till they just touch the ground at the tips – in fact, acting as a kind of support to the tail feathers, and keeping them from being soiled by contact with the floor.

ACTION AND MOTION

These can scarcely be described in words – they should be seen to be understood and appreciated; but this short description would be quite incomplete did I not allude to these most valuable artistic additions, which give so much dash and style to the "Fantail Shaker". In the first place, let me here observe that action and motion must not be confounded the one with the other.

Motion is found in very ordinary Fantails, and consists of a constant tremulous movement of the neck to and fro to a greater or less degree. It is only when this is combined with *action*, which depends solely on the exercise of the limb power, that those beautiful and graceful performances are achieved which display the charms to which I have already alluded. The birds best able to accomplish these feats are those which have the power of standing, as it were, on the very tips of their claws with jaunty agility; hence proceeds a spring–like motion by which the whole body seems in sudden turns to be twisted first to the right then to the left, and then again round and round in small circles in rapid succession, the chest being in the meantime well projecting, the tail very erect, and the head and neck seemingly beating time to the dance then proceeding.

I know scarcely any sight more pretty in the pigeon fancy than to see one of these high–bred and well–trained little beauties go through this pirouette–like accomplishment. To realise all that is meant by the action and motion of a good bird must be left to **optical evidence** rather than words.

A DETAILED DESCRIPTION

A few years ago might be seen at the same Show and in the same class side by side, birds of totally different type and character, the one, known as the English type, being "all tail", and the other, called the Scottish type, "all action". It is regrettable that there should have been so much diversity of opinion as to the most desirable type of bird to perpetuate. Happily much of this antagonistic feeling is fast dying out, the votaries of English *v.* Scots and Scots *v.* English being now pretty well agreed that the "perfect" Fantail should be represented by the following points and properties:

The *Size* should be small.

Shape of body, round, with back slightly hollowed in the centre. The chest should be broad, round and free from any hollowness, except a slight parting in the centre. The length of back should harmonize with the length of neck so as to enable the head to rest closely on the cushion.

The *neck* should be thin and swanlike, tapering off as it approaches the head.

Carriage erect, with the head thrown well back, and resting closely on the cushion.

The *chest* should be brought well forward.

Figure 2.4 'A' Early Fantail after Willughby

Figure 2.5 ' B' Exhibition type appeared around 1900 or earlier.

Early Fantails showing the development of the Tail

The first fantails had enlarged tail , but only half the size of the present day birds (see A). From around 1900 the "fan" was quite distinctive (see B)

17

Figure 2.6 White Fantail Cock : *Dandy Prince,*
Best in Show, 1919.

Figure 2.7 Yellow Laced Fantail
**Cup winner at Club Show in 1919. These historical pictures show the
tremendous development of the fantail**

The *tail* should be carried well up, evenly balanced, i.e., with a series of convulsive jerkings or twitchings of the neck, not dropping over the head, or hanging loosely to the right or the left.

Motion adds much to the graceful movements. The Fantail should appear as standing on tiptoe, walk in a jaunty manner, and with a series of convulsive jerkings or twitchings of the neck. The *head* should be small, slightly depressed, but not flat.

The *eye* should be bull or dark hazel in whites and saddlebacks, and pearl or gravel in other colours.

The *beak* thin and about half an inch in length.

Beak wattle and *eye cere* very small and fine in texture.

Legs of moderate length (short rather than long).

The *tail* should be circular, and only slightly concave; the feathers should be long, broad and evenly set, closely overlapping each other, and showing no "gape" in the centre of the tail.

COLOURS

Fantails are of all colours: the whites, however, are both the most popular and attractive; but blacks, blues, and silvers are numerous and of good standard points, as are also some Turbit-shouldered and saddle-marked specimens. Laced-feathered Fans have been produced of remarkably good character; but some of these are feather-footed, which, according to standard requirements, is a great fault. Now and again specimens are found peak-crested, showing a probable Mookee ancestry, for these Indian pigeons very much resemble Fantails in tremulous action – chest-fulness, arched neck, narrowness of skull, and a tendency also to width of tail; moreover, in common with the Mookee, the Fantail owes much to Eastern cultivation.

The Fantail, if not too high bred, is an excellent breeder and feeder, and is very prolific. It is the custom of fanciers of high-class specimens to cut off the tails of their show birds during the breeding season.

A club for the Fantail was established in 1886 but did not prosper. In 1889 a new organisation was founded, and there is a present day Fantail Club in the UK and many abroad. There are *standards* laid down for Exhibition and Indian Fantails. Both are complete standards for Fantail pigeons.

HOUSING

The proper housing of Fantails is important. It would be madness to attempt to keep Show birds in houses with "flights" that are greatly exposed.

PERCHES

A long–felt want has been a suitable perch for Fantails, one upon which they could poise naturally and peacefully, and without breaking or soiling their chief adornment, the tail. I therefore direct attention to the illustration which shows a "stage perch" which in practice will be found much more suitable for the variety than the fittings one sees in Fantail lofts generally.

THE ATTRACTION

Besides providing an interesting and fascinating hobby fantails are gentle and attractive birds to keep. They breed fairly easily and become extremely tame. My own birds are so well domesticated that I have to be very careful going into the loft to avoid treading on them. They have no objection to being handled and when feeding young they show no resentment to the humans who come to view.

CHAPTER 3

THE VARIETIES

DIFFERENT TYPES

From what has been stated earlier it will be seen that there are different types of fantails:

1.   **Exhibition Fantail**
This is the European type fantail which has been in existence for hundreds of years. It is also known as the Modern Fantail. Besides normal feathering there is the *laced* variety, the *Silkie* and the *Frizzle* .

2.   **Indian Fantail**
This is a larger type of fantail which is quite different in style and feathering. Besides having a crest at the back of the head it also has feathered legs.

Another difference is the manner of standing; the Indian should not rear back and shake like the Exhibition Fantail.

3.   **Garden Fantail (or Feral Pigeon with a fan tail)**

Garden Fantails are very popular, but there is a danger of crosses from stray pigeons and this results in very strange mixtures of size, style, colours and variations in the all-important tail. Some have what has been called a " shovel tail" which is a large, but does not erect properly to meet the

21

back of the head.These are large birds and nice in a garden however,they do not exhibit the style of the thorough bred fantail. For this reason there is a tendency for garden fantails to be treated as pets and not to have any form of *standard.*

Silkie & Frizzle Fantails

As noted ,other variations to be found are in the **type of feather on the pigeon.** There is the **Silkie** type where the feathers are soft and fluffy or the **Frizzle** when the feathers curl; both forms are often seen in poultry , but are not seen frequently in Fantails ; as fancy birds they provide an added dimension for those who like the unusual.A *laced* type also exists which may be a cross of the Normal and the Silkie.

THE ABBREVIATED STANDARDS

For a full description of the standards readers are referred to the book *Fancy Pigeon Standards* published for the National Pigeon Association.

The summaries that follow are taken from *Exhibition and Flying Pigeons* by Harry Wheeler:

STANDARD FOR THE EXHIBITION WHITE FANTAIL

Head: Small, fine and snaky, free from peak or shell.
Beak: Thin , flesh coloured and of medium length, the upper mandible slightly curved at the tip.
Beak Wattles: Small and fine in texture.
Eyes: Dark hazel or bull, with Cere, fine and flesh coloured.
Neck: Nicely curved and tapering off as it approaches the head; length of neck corresponding with the length of back, so as to enable the head to rest closely on the cushion.
Body: Small and round, back slightly hollowed in centre, length of back to be in proportion to the length of neck, enabling the

head to rest on the cushion with ease. The rump to be of sufficient size and strength to balance the tail evenly. The chest to be round like a ball.

Cushion and Tail: Cushion full and massive, the feathers at the feathers below the hocks. Feet, small and fine and neat, bright red in colour.

Carriage: The bird stands on tip-toe and walks with a jaunty air, front and back overlapping each other extending well up the tail feathers. Tail slightly concave and circular, closely filled with long, broad, evenly set feathers well overlapping each other.

Legs and Feet: Legs moderately short, not stilty, and free from feathers with head thrown back in a graceful manner, resting closely on the cushion. Body to be upright, in a straight line with legs, wings set fairly low and closely braced. Flights preferably short, just clearing the lowest tail feather, and almost meeting at the tips.

Tail: Carried well up, not being allowed to droop or incline forward.

Legs: Well apart, the hocks being forced forward by the action of the body.

Note: : **The above is the** Standard **for Whites. In only the beak , cere and eye colour will the** standards **vary for other colours.**

NOTE : **Colours** : Laces, Saddles, Blacks, Blues, Silvers, Powdered Silvers, Reds, Yellows, Duns and Chequers. All the above coloured Fantails receive from 5 to 15 extra points over the Whites.

STANDARD FOR THE INDIAN FANTAIL

The Indian Fantail is much larger than the Exhibition Fantail and more than double the length; its head is crested, and the legs are grouse legged.

The species could have originated from the early Fantails in India – the breed that probably made the Exhibition Fantail we know today. If the Indian Fantail is to prosper in Britain, it needs a few keen fanciers who could "fix the breed", because at present it varies so much in size, stance and tail.

The description is as follows:

Colours: In most cases splashes, and unusual mixed colours. Self colours, when exhibited, to be judged according to the soundness of colour.

Size: Large, and the larger the better.

Stance: Stands normally; the head is not carried back, as in other Fantails.

Head: Large and full, with little or no "shake".

Neck: Short and full.

Body: Large and round.

Back: Short and wide.

Tail: Large and upright; the longer and more upright, the better.

Feet and Legs: Legs medium length; feet stand firm with no standing on tiptoe.

Foot Feathers: Grouse legged, but can be longer. All toes should be well covered with feather.

Crests: There is a peak as in an Archangel, or it can be a small shell, the size of a thumb nail.

Eye Colour: Other than pearl is preferred.

Figure 3.1 Indian Fantail

THE COLOURS – EXHIBITION FANTAILS

As indicated the main colour is white. However, over the years many other colours have developed:

1. Blacks

The colour should be jet black with a beetle green sheen on the hackle, possibly also with purple sheen. There should be no other colours to mar the effect. Eye should be pearl or orange with dark ceres and beak and toenails should be black.

2. Blues

These are a soft slate or lavender blue, evenly coloured and without any foul feathering. Eye ,beak and toenails as for Blacks.

3. Chequers

Birds have a special colour pattern on the wings.There should be good and even markings throughout with the light colour looking like a T on the wing coverts. Eyes , beak and toenails to match the basic colour such as Red, Blue and Brown.

4. Creams

The colour is a darkish cream with no other colours. The exception is the neck hackle which would show a metallic, darker sheen, especially marked in the cock.

5. Duns

Duns are a brown colour usually a greyish or reddish shade.

6. Reds

This colour should be a bright chestnut red without bluish marks.

7. Silver and Powdered Silver

Both colours should look like a metal silver, but in the

powdered bird there is light powdering with a whitish colour.

8. Yellows

This should be a rich yellow, quite bright, deep and evenly distributed.Eyes should be orange.

Other colours exist , including Almond, Brown, Grizzle and even Andalusian after the fowl of that name which is a slate colour with darker lacing.

Note: Some standards specify the colour of the legs, beak and toe nails; generally speaking the natural colours should be matched with the plumage. Thus a Black Fantail would have black legs and toe nails, whereas a light colour such as white , silver, and yellow would have white or horn as the appropriate matching colour.

OTHER VARIATIONS

For show purposes there are other variations:

1. **Saddles** – a coloured wing shield on white background.

2. **Markings** – tail is coloured.

There are also Splashes with splashes of different colour , and mismarks for those with uneven colour patterns.

Figure 3.2   A White Fantail (H W Rogers)

Figure 3.3 *Saddle* Fantail (H W Rogers)

27

CHAPTER 4

THE PIGEON HOUSE

SOUND & SUITABLE HOUSING ESSENTIAL

Any "hole and corner" will not do for housing pigeons. It is next to impossible to keep even the most common and hardy varieties in health and vigour in cramped-up, draughty, and unsanitary abodes. Better by far not to keep pigeons at all, than keep then in miserable places. It must be remembered that health and comfort go hand in hand in pigeon life pretty much as they do among other classes of stock, and among our human selves.

Essentials
The essentials of a habitation for pigeons are:

1. It should be perfectly dry (i.e. waterproof)
2. Free from damp and draught
3. Well ventilated

It may not be generally known that pigeons will stand almost any amount of cold, providing the atmosphere is dry, and draughts are rigidly excluded from their dwellings. Such, however, is the case, and it should be carefully noted. Pigeons – like pigs – have a great aversion to high winds, so that in siting a pigeon house it will be necessary to keep this in mind.

Disused stables, hay lofts, barns, garden houses, and other outbuildings may be transformed into pigeonries. The essential **requirements** for inclusion in building a loft are discussed below and should be considered.

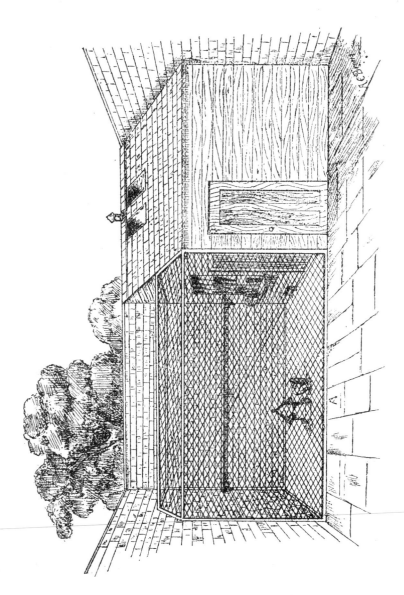

Figure 4.1 Model Aviary
A lean-to shed which may be adapted for a single wall site.

PLANNING A PIGEON HOUSE
The Lean-To

The back garden is a capital site for the erection of a small pigeonry. A brick or stone wall may be profitably utilised to form a part of the place it is proposed to construct. An examination of the sketch of house and flight (fig. 4.1) will clearly illustrate its adaptability to such a site, and assist greatly in conveying the idea how best the thing may be done.

It therefore only remains for me to give the necessary details for the construction of such a house. Firstly, then, we will suppose the available ground space to be, say, twenty-four feet wide. This should be apportioned as shown on the ground plan Fig. 3) house ten feet and flight fourteen feet. A suitable depth for this width is ten feet, so that you have a house ten feet square, with suitable flight, and capable of accommodating during the breeding season – according to the variety kept – from four to eight pairs of stud birds, and at other times from fifteen to twenty-five birds.

It should be observed that on economy of cost this house is designed as simply as possible, but a more ornate structure may be conceived by anyone wishing to put up something artistic.

Given a substantial wall as a basis for operations, I prefer wooden structures generally, both on account of cost, and as tending to increase the comfort and well-being of the birds. One of the great secrets of pigeon keeping is knowing how to construct the house for their reception.

After examining the sketch, and without reading the text, nineteen people out of every twenty would probably "run up" a flimsy match-boarded shed, and imagine they had provided accommodation suitable for the purpose, but this should not be the way of an experienced fancier. Firstly, then, it must be *double covered* (i.e. boarded outside and insulated inside), the outer covering being of three-quarters of an inch and insulating ply or similar inside.feather edged boards, properly rebated and nailed to the framing. The inner side should be boarded with ply or hard boards and insulated between with suitable insulating material. The floor should be laid with three-quarters of an inch batten floor boards – grooved and tongued – and properly nailed to the timbers below. The roof, too, should be boarded and then lined inside. Cover the roof with heavy duty roofing felt which can be tarred regularly.

Perches, and fittings generally, are treated of fully else-where.

VENTILATION

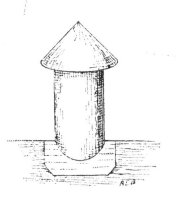

Air Pipe for ventilation

Ventilation must not be for-gotten, and is effectually attained by means of a cone-covered pipe in the roof, This permits the foul air to escape without down draught, or too free a current.

The means of getting in and out for the birds, if properly regu-lated, is generally sufficient to ensure an ample supply of fresh air, but in very warm weather both window and door should be opened.

A SAFETY LOBBY

On the ground plan a small lobby is shown – the utility of which may be questioned – but as "prevention is better than cure", this is added with a view of securing an entry to the flight from either the outside or from the house itself, without risking an escape of the inmates. An alternative plan, having the entrance to the flight at the point marked A, may in some cases be adopted, but if the variety kept be naturally wild or timid, I strongly advise the adoption of my "safety lobby" arrangement as depicted in the plan of the shed.

POP HOLES

The most convenient means of the birds getting from the house to flight and *vice versa* is a stock sash with sliding lights, one square of which should be fitted with a small door, to be used as a means of getting in and out in very bad weather, and when it is necessary that the window should be closed.

MAIN AIM

A house constructed on this principle should give satisfaction. No matter what the weather may be – and we do get some bad weather in this country – such a pigeonry will be little influenced by its vagaries. A somewhat lengthy experience teaches me, that pigeons cannot reasonably be expected to thrive in their habitation is subject to many and frequent changes of temperature. I cannot, therefore, too strongly **condemn** the use of galvanized sheeting for the roofing of pigeon houses *unless* lined on the inside with stout boards or insulating material. As is well-known, metal is readily influenced by both heat and cold, so that a house roofed with it, would, say, on a sunny day in autumn, be almost unbearable; whereas at night time, with a fast falling thermometer, it would be the other extreme. There need be no wonder that roup and kindred maladies are so prevalent in pigeon houses so constructed.

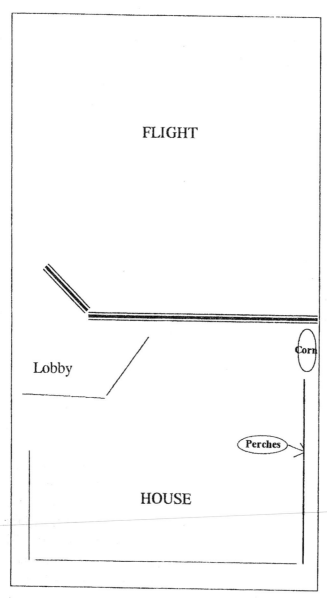

A plan for the Pigeon House in Fig 4.10

THE DE–LUXE HOUSE

A convenient kind of house for a fancier wishing to indulge his hobby beyond the limits of fig. 4.1 is that illustrated by fig. 4.3, and which I have named the "Duplex". Such a house – the dimensions of which are given on the ground plan (fig. 4.4) – may be fitted to a garden wall or detached from any other building. Therein may be kept some forty or fifty or more birds, without unduly overcrowding them, and the arrangement of the compartments allows the sexes to be divided – as they should be in all cases – during the non–breeding season. I have just said that a pigeonry of this size is capable of accommodating forty or fifty birds, and so it is in an ordinary way, but during the breeding season the number must be greatly reduced, if success is to be attained.

I would remark here, as elsewhere, that one of the most common pitfalls in pigeon culture, is – attempting to breed from pigeons that are unduly crowded. During the breeding season, if at no other time, ample space *must* be provided for each pair of stud birds.

This house should be built of similar materials to fig. 4.1, the additional features being the duplicate compartments, and an overhead loft for the reception of a few pairs of common pigeons to be used as "feeders", and which, be it noted, should have entire liberty.

Numerous modifications of this plan may be suggested, the chief of which are:– (1) each compartment may be reduced to nine feet square, and a pen room, food store, etc., thereby provided; (2) the passage or gangway between the flights may be dispensed with, and the space utilised for an extra flight to as third compartment; (3) a single door may be substituted for the two outer ones, and inner doors provided to each compartment; (4) a skirting board from 12 to 18 inches high may be placed around each flight.

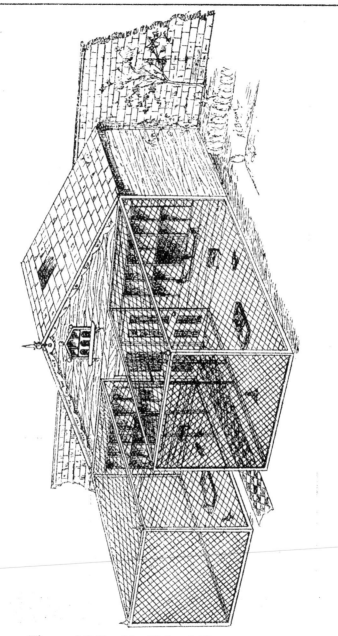

Figure 4.3 Double flighted Pigeon House.

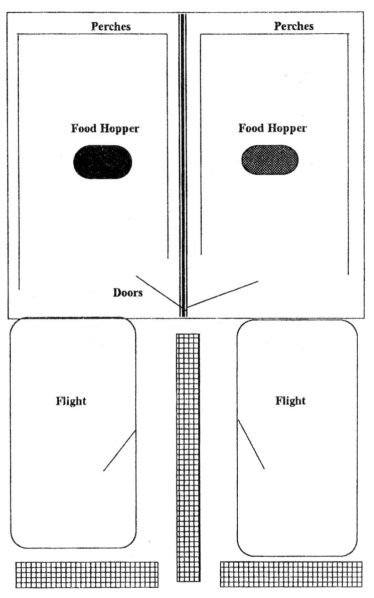

Figure 4.4 Sketch for Double Flight Pigeon House
(not to scale–see text)

If my plan be adopted in its entirety, I recommend that the passage be enclosed with wire–netting, so as to reduce to a minimum any chances of an escape of the birds. It will be observed that a landing–stage is shown against each open window, which, by the way, may be either a sash light or sliding window. This landing stage should be about nine inches wide, one inch thick, nicely rounded off at the ends, and firmly secured to brackets of wood or iron. Another of similar dimensions should be affixed inside the house.

This illustration shows the "grit box" *under* the ouside landing stage, this being, in my opinion, the most suitable place for it that can be found.

THE LARGE SCALE OPERATION

Having dealt with fanciers "in a small way", I will next pass to the ambitious person, one whose resources include having ample ground space, sufficient funds, and a desire to put up something that will be both useful and ornamental, and I should like it to be clearly understood that the style of aviary I am next about to describe is the one I advocate in all cases in which it is possible to carry out the design, and I may remark in passing that this is the principle upon which my own range of houses – fourteen in number – are constructed.

It would be impossible to illustrate the whole in one picture except as a bird's eye view, I have therefore no alternative but to give a sketch of a section only (fig. 4.6), and ask readers to apply the description to the structure generally. The ground plan (fig. 4.7) will aid in solving this difficulty.

A range of ten houses (five aside) will supply the requirements of the majority of breeders, still, there are I know, not a few so deeply engrossed in the pursuit that double that number would not be too abundant. Be that as it may, the general design remains the same, so that the number and size of compartments can be regulated by the inclination and means of the breeder.

To the right of the show room I have added a house with covered flight, this being another important accessory in the design of an extensive pigeonry, and one that may be used either as a convalescent ward, or for the reception of birds that have been recently washed, or as the general habitation of varieties for which a covered area is needed.

The general details of construction already given will enable any practical carpenter to run up a range of houses of this kind with satisfaction to himself, to which may be added a little fuller explanation, applicable more especially to the range of houses now being considered.

Bricks and mortar will have to be freely used in providing a substantial and suitable wall on three sides of the square or parellelogram, as the case may be. I am an advocate for a **cavity wall**, the advantages of which are (1) dryness; (2) may be used as a means of ventilating the houses; (3) the pillars, being internal, a much cleaner and better job can be made than when the masonry is *en masse*. The wall should also extend along the ends of houses as shown in the sketch. The fronts should be framed with sills and plates, and boarded in like manner as described elsewhere.

The windows should be sliding lights, so that the atmos–

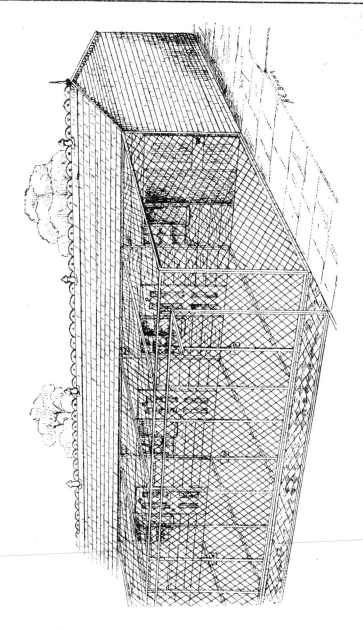

Figure 4.6 Large Scale House with flights

phere of the houses may be regulated according to the season of the year and the vagaries of the weather. The height of windows and means of **in** and **out** must be arranged according to the requirements of the variety of pigeon it is proposed to go in for.

The doors of each house should be centrally placed, in order that the internal fittings may be conveniently arranged, and all four corners available for the use of stud birds during the breeding season. The doors may be either one inch "ledged", or "framed and panelled". The roof in shape may be either "span" or "lean–to", the former being, perhaps, more artistic and better adapted for general use.

The gangway in this case would, I think, be more appro-priately termed the promenade, and many a keen fancier will take delight in using this space as a vantage ground for viewing the birds and studying their habits and ever–varying characteristics.

For reasons already explained, this space should be en-closed with wirework or it could be covered over to give a sheltered area for observing even in wet weather.

It will be observed that the framework of flights are shown incomplete, i.e. without cross stays and supports. This plan has been adopted in all illustrations with a view of causing as little obstruction as possible in the elucidation of each house.

Another thing that should be mentioned is the wirework of flights, the chief points to bear in mind being (1) strength; (2) durability; (3) the exclusion of cats, rats, and small birds. Netting of 18 gauge and 1 inch mesh answers all these requirements, and is therefore the most suitable.

HOUSE WITH COVERED FLIGHT

Fantails need specially arranged houses, and if an outer area or flight can be added the better will the birds thrive. I have, therefore, designed a house with a covered flight which I can recommend as suitable for fantails and other varieties that would quickly deteriorate in feather if not protected from heavy rains, high winds, and other inclemencies.

40

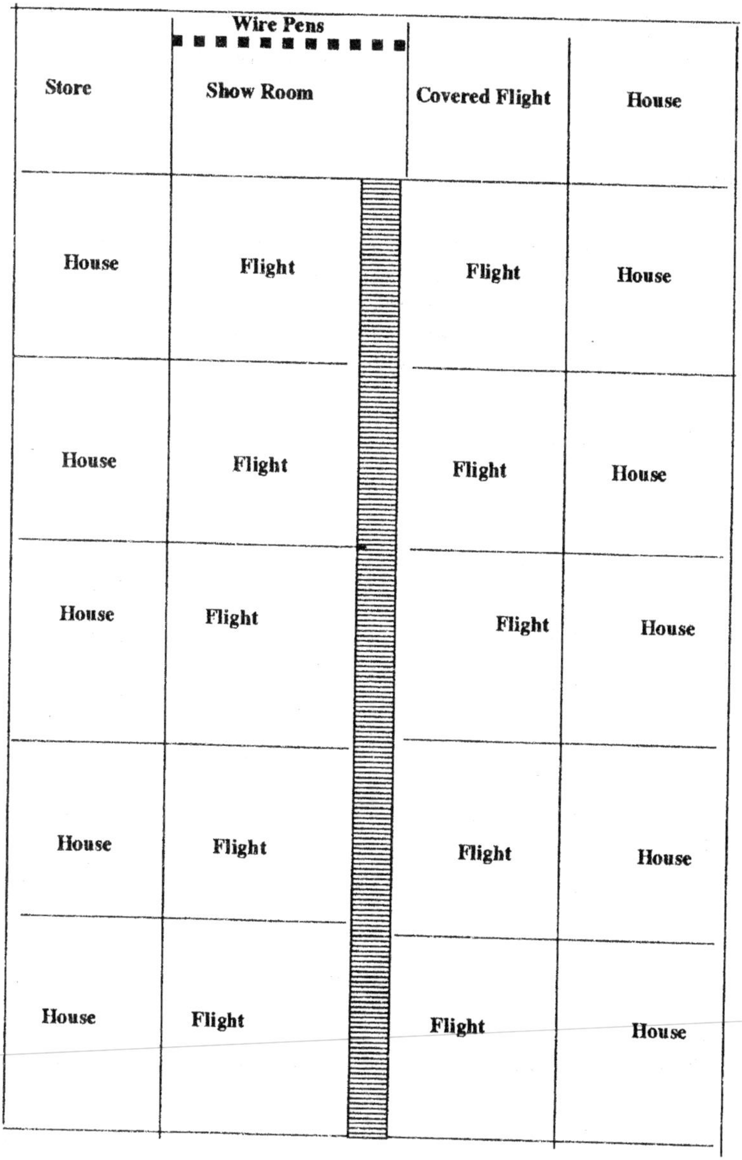

Store	Show Room	Covered Flight	House
House	Flight	Flight	House
House	Flight	Flight	House
House	Flight	Flight	House
House	Flight	Flight	House
House	Flight	Flight	House

Wire Pens

Figure 4.7 Plan of **Part** of Large scale Pigeon House.
Not to scale ; only an approximate guide to layout.

An examination of the illustration (figure 4.8) shows the whole arrangement as a "lean–to", so that if a tolerably high wall is at hand a structure of this kind can be put up at small cost. My description of the construction of fig. 4.1 is, in part, applicable to this erection also, the particular features of which are its suitability for:–

1.Fantails;

2.Pouters, Trumpeters, and all feather–legged varieties;

3. Red and Yellow Pigeons, and others that need protection from the scorching and bleaching rays of the sun;

4 Short–faced Tumblers and other varieties that must, as certain periods of the year, be kept without access to an outer flight;
and

5. Its adaptability with but slight alteration for *any* variety.

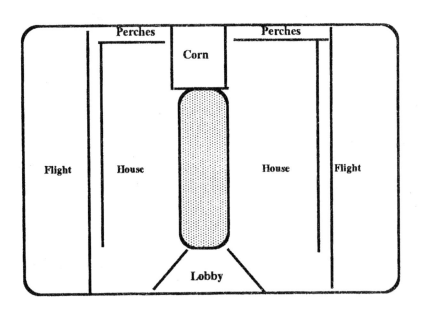

Figure 4.8 Plan for Covered Flights

It is intended that the window in front should be a sliding one, and run the whole length of each house, so that – according to the exigencies of the weather – it may be wide open (as shown in the illustration), partly open, or shut. Thus air may be freely admitted or excluded at will.

The lobby, as shown on the ground plan (fig. 4.8) serves as a store for corn, show hampers, and the many other essentials needed for successful pigeon keeping.

The arrangement of perches must be governed by the variety kept, the requirements of each being full explained elsewhere. A ready means of "in" and "out" is the sashlight as shown in the sketch.

The top of the "flight" should be covered with boarding eight or nine inches wide, half an inch or five–eighths of an inch in thickness, fluted along the outside edges, and fixed with a space of a quarter of an inch or three–eighths of an inch between each board. An arrangement of this kind will be found to answer admirably. Through the interspaces light and air are freely admitted, as well as the exhilarating influences of the rays of the sun, without the deleterious effects that would be produced by more direct contact.

On ventilation, also, my plan for a covered "area or flight" will prove effectual. Two or three stout boards should be affixed along the entire length of the bottom of the flight to screen the birds, and keep dry the floor from beating rains. Constructed on this principle, the flight will always be dry and warm – never hot, never cold – essential   in the successful management of any of the breeds for which this house is intended.

It will be observed that the ends of each flight are shown "broken". Thus, they may be of any length, according to the space at command.

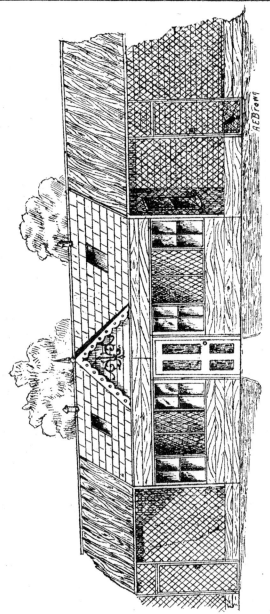

Figure 4.9 Covered Aviary for Fantails
Keeps birds protected from elements

THE MOST SUITABLE ASPECT

Sunshine and warmth are as desirable as protection from strong easterly or westerly winds, and blinding northern snow-storms, but it must be remembered that it is quite possible to have too much of even a *good thing.* . Whilst granting that **direct** northerly and easterly aspects are to be generally avoided, I must, point out that pigeon houses may be so arranged in these positions so as to minimise the drawbacks. To my mind the construction of the house and the selection of the variety it is proposed to go in for, are of far greater importance than the exact position of the space at command.

Strange as it may seem, I have, year after year, successfully reared some most precocious youngsters in houses facing due north. It is not often one has the choice of "quarters", but I may, nevertheless, remark that south-easterly or south-westerly aspects are – all things considered – the most suitable, thus avoiding extremes.

ARRANGEMENT OF INTERIORS

The illustration (fig. 4.10), represents internal fittings of various houses. To the left is shown an arrangement of perches and breeding boxes that will be found applicable for most breeds.

INTERNAL FITTINGS

SELECT SUITABLE PERCHES

Perches are of much importance, and need more than passing comment. For Carriers, Barbs, Turbits, Owls, Nuns, Magpies, Dragons, Antwerps, and clear-legged varieties generally, I have found perches of the kind shown in Figure 4.11 most suitable.

45

Figure 4.10   Internal Arrangements of Pigeon House

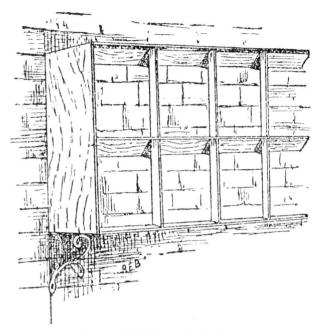

Figure 4.11 Boxed–in Perches

Suitable for those birds that are best separated fom each other.

The advantages of these are: (1) only one bird can occupy each compartment; (2) consequent freedom from fighting; (3) they are practically self–cleaning. The dimensions may be varied a little to suit the different varieties, but a good *general* size for each division, is 14 in. high by 11 in. wide. Perches of this kind should be not more than $2\,^3/_4$ in. deep, made out of $^1/_2$ in. red deal or pitch pine, and fitted with slanting boards at the back (only), about $4\,^1/_2$ in. or 5 in. wide, to carry off the droppings. They should be placed about 12 inches from the wall.

The same kind of perch may be used for other varieties, the size of pedestal being regulated by the size of birds which are kept.

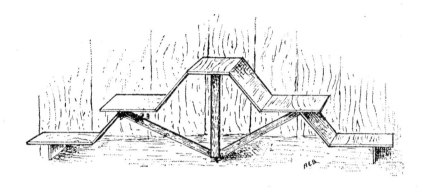

Figure 4.12 Platform perches most suitable for Fantails
These avoid damage to the tail..

SPECIALS FOR FANTAILS

For Fantails, a long–felt want has been a suitable perch, one on which they can rest and poise without damaging their chief property – the tail – and without too frequent an attack from a quarrelsome neighbour. I have therefore much satisfaction in being able to introduce a perch of novel design and one that will befit the peculiarities and vagaries of this attractive pigeon.

This perch or platform being a portable one, it can readily be arranged to suit the exigencies of almost any style of pigeon house, and as a guide to those desirous of trying my invention, I may say that the height from the floor line to the topmost platform should be 2 feet , each platform being 8 or 9 inches square, the lower ones 6 inches from the floor, and others 9 inches apart.

The same kind of perch, (slightly reduced in height), may be used for Trumpeters.

48

Low shelves are also useful resting places for Fantails, Pouters, Jacobins, and Trumpeters, the great drawback being, that nearly every Pigeon is so much elated with its own importance, that it is constantly striving for more territory than the owner thinks it ought to occupy. Shelves (with or without divisions) may also be used for Short-faced Tumblers and a few other of the smaller breeds.

PERCHES IN THE "FLIGHTS"

These should be arranged in convenient positions in accordance with the requirements of each variety, care being taken that they do not intersect each other – like so many telephone wires – in all directions, and thereby prevent that freedom of movement which is so conducive to the well-being of pigeons generally.

As a rule, the most suitable perch for the "area or flight" is a long narrow rail about $3/_4$ in. thick and 3 in. wide. Perches of this simple kind may be fixed on brackets of wood or iron, around the flight at various distances and heights in accordance with the exigencies of the situation.

THE SHOW OR PEN ROOM

This carries me to the show, or pen room, and a most interesting place it is too, either when filled with a bevy of show birds, the choicest specimens of a season's breeding, or later on, when the walls are decorated with prize cards, of victories won. The sketch illustrates the internal arrangement of this room. It will be observed that the cages or pens are placed in rows along the back wall, this being, all things considered, the most convenient position for them. These pens will be found most useful, and, if the stud is a large one, rarely be without occupants, for they may be used for a variety of purposes such as : (1) confining sick birds; (2) preparing birds for show; (3) making a

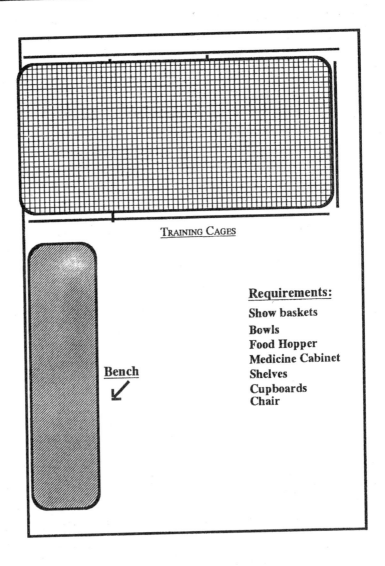

Figure 4.13 Plan for Show– or Penning Room

critical examination of any, with a view of purchasing or selling; (4) matching up the stud birds, and so on.

The show hampers in use, may be stowed away either under or above the pens; in either position they will keep dry, and be ready for use at short notice.

The table will be found useful when washing birds, and otherwise preparing them for the show pen. A corn bin should also be located in this "snuggery", as well as other little items. If kept clean and tidy, many a happy hour may be spent in a little room of this kind.

The store to the left (shown on the ground plan, fig. 4.7), will be found a useful receptacle for stowing away breeding boxes, show hampers, other requisites, and for the storage of the food supply.

Above the show room and covered flight, may be built a good roomy loft, for the accommodation of "feeders". This should be well constructed.

Figure 14.14 The Show Basket

PREPARATION FOR THE SHOW PEN

In preparing pigeons for shows it is necessary to accustom them to being confined in the show pen; such training is essential with birds that are by nature shy and timid. *"Carriage "* training is vital so that the fantail 'shows off' in the show pen.

Condition , too, is a point upon which some judges lay considerable stress, and I frankly own that I give the preference to clean well-conditioned birds, providing, of course, that the properties of the variety are *combined* with cleanliness and bloom.

The advantages of the modern show system are many. Fanciers and breeders from all parts of the country can meet for the mutual exchange of ideas and the comparison of their stock. Apart from the glory of prize winning – much practical knowledge is obtainable, even if the verdict of the judge is averse. On the other hand, if successful in the show, the probability is you will be fired with zeal, and go on to greater wins.

CATCHING PIGEONS

Pigeons, being by nature shy and timid, it is best to approach them gently and kindly; especially when it is desired to catch one of them. Avoid scuttling or blustering about.

A bird net of the kind used by fishermen, in landing their spoil, is frequently used, but an arrangement of this kind may inflict injury unless due care is taken.

A much better plan is to quietly enter the house or loft after dark and by the aid of torch select the bird required. If a bird has be captured during the day time, it should be skilfully manoeuvred into a corner, and approached expeditiously but quietly. To attract the bird's attention, and keep it under control, one hand should be raised in accordance with the movements of the bird, and then caught with the other hand.

Usually fantails are quite tame so they can be caught up without difficulty.

HOLDING A PIGEON

If an experienced fancier is observed it will be seen that the legs should be placed between the first and second fingers, with the breast of the bird resting in the palm of the hand, and the wings secured in position with the fingers and thumb as shown in the sketch. Held in this manner the wildest pigeon is quickly at ease, and may be readily examined.

PACKAGES

Boxes, hampers or baskets are used for sending pigeons to the Shows, and I am sorry to say that some of the packages so used by exhibitors, who really ought to know better, are of a most unsuitable kind – boxes, for instance, that are so small and ill-ventilated, that the wonder to me is that the inmates survive their journey.

WASHING

For light coloured birds washing is essential. The proce-dure follows that adopted for all exhibition birds , whether poultry , canaries or pigeons.

Three bowls are recommended:

1.One with fairly hot water , but not unbearable, in which washing up liquid is added and the fantail is given a good soaking ; where necessary scrub the really soiled wing and tail feathers.

2. The remaining bowls containing clean warm water for rinsing out the soap from the feathers.

Avoid the bird's eyes because detergents can irritate.

Once clean the main moisture should be dried with a towel and the process finished off with a hair dryer or a heated cage where a steady , but not excessive temperature is used.

CHAPTER 5
GENERAL MANAGEMENT

DILIGENCE IS ESSENTIAL

It matters little how much money has been spent in the building of aviaries or in the selection of stock if the general management is wrong. I can imagine no more deplorable sight to a genuine fancier than an inspection of another's loft, in which chaos and disorder reign supreme. On the other hand I can speak from experience of the pleasure derivable from the inspection of a stud of pigeons, where order and cleanliness are discernible throughout.

FOOD HOPPERS

Feeding naturally claims first attention. This should be done systematically. There are now many sorts of feeding troughs and hoppers, in the construction of some of which great ingenuity has been displayed. The majority are contrived on the self–supplying principle, so that the birds may have a constant supply of grain, and feed at will. Now the first essentials are to keep the corn dry and clean and prevent waste.

FOOD & FEEDING

Having provided a proper hopper we might next pass on to the consideration of food suitable for the different seasons, but as this subject is fully dealt with in a separate chapter, I shall briefly state here that a **mixture of tick beans, grey peas, and corn** will be found the best general food for most varieties, omitting the beans and adding rather more corn for the smaller birds.

THE BEST WINTER FEED

It may be taken as a good general rule that as a winter "feed" for most varieties a mixture of beans, maple peas and mixed corn, in about equal proportion, will be found suitable. As the breeding season comes round this winter diet must be changed.

Wheat   Peas

Beans   Maize

Figure 5.1 Basic Foods – wheat, maize, peas and beans.
The above taken from a standard Pigeon Mix available from a pet store.

DIET FOR THE BREEDING SEASON

Now the proper time to *commence* changing the diet of pigeons is soon after the putting of the birds together, and certainly before the first batch of youngsters are expected. This then supplies an ample supply of pigeon's milk with which to start the newly-hatched squabs into existence.

We will suppose the winter feed to have been a mixture of beans, peas, and mixed corn, in which case it will be advisable to *gradually* omit the beans, and as gradually increase the supply of mixed corn and 'extras' such as a small quantity of sound Spanish canary seed, and a little millet seed. Some fanciers feed small-sized poultry pellets, but these are very much an acquired taste and my fantails will not take to them; however, they do eat parrot food and crumbly bread. During the very hot weather green food, such as cabbages, lettuces etc., may be sparingly given with advantage. Pigeons eat these greens with much avidity.

Unsuitable Foods

Maize, barley and hemp seed may be given to pigeons, but very sparingly; they tend to overheat the system and to fatten.

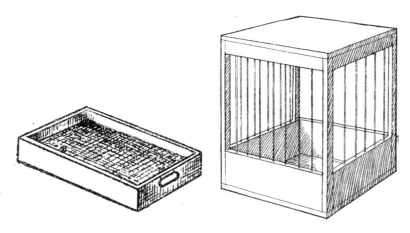

Figure 5.2 Different types of Bird Bath

THE BATH

The bath is of vital importance in the outfit of a well-managed pigeonry, though the desirability of its regular use is not sufficiently recognised by the majority of fanciers. Water is cheap and plentiful, there is therefore no excuse on the score of cost for withholding the bath. Pigeons are naturally clean in habit, and if the opportunity is afforded them they will take a bath, say, every forty-eight hours. Spraying with water is also appreciated by the pigeons , especially on a hot day .

It may, however, be laid down as a good general rule, that a bath should be provided twice or three times a week during the spring and summer months, and once a week during the winter. A good form of bath is made of galvanised metal or of plastic. A shallow container made for the base of a small barrel or large plant pot is ideal. This is the type I use.

It is most amusing to watch pigeons bathe. Apparently they take delight in wallowing in the water, expanding their wings, loosening the arrangement of feathers and then, when the plumage is well-nigh saturated, they give a vigorous shake, and the water at once becomes quite white and milky with the scurf thrown off from the skin of the bird – proof plenty that the bath is an absolute necessity for pigeons.

SALT AND OTHER REQUISITES

In addition to a plentiful supply of food and water, pigeons need a supply of sharp, gritty sand to assist in the digestion of their food. Salt must also be provided, but as pigeons are passionately fond of this saline, care should be taken not to allow them to partake of it too freely. Calcareous matter, to furnish material for the eggshells and assist in the bone formation of the young birds is also necessary.

Figure 5.3 The Grit Box

The advantages of placing grit in a box of this kind are threefold:–

(1)   Cleanliness and freedom from waste.

(2)   Protection from the weather.

(3)   Readiness of access.

It must be noted that I recommend that the "grit box" should be placed in the "area or flight" (in a sheltered position) in preference to being relegated to one corner of the house or loft and thereby losing its utility, by becoming a receptacle for dust, dirt, loose feathers, etc. Boxes can be readily made by anyone possessed of the most elementary knowledge of amateur joinery, but as there are doubtless many breeders who have no desire to risk their fingers and thumbs, I would just say that these boxes can be made by any joiner or carpenter.

COVERING FOR THE FLOOR OF THE HOUSE

For covering the floor of the pigeon *house* , nothing is better than wood shavings or sawdust. This is readily obtainable in most towns, and when fresh from the mills it acts as a powerful deodorant and disinfectant. For the very centre of the floor of the house (i.e. where the food hopper is placed) I like sharp gritty sand, so that any food that may be scattered by the birds is not wasted. Another advantage in using sand, as indicated, will be found when the young birds emerge from their nests, for in picking up the food they also learn to pick up the grit.

COVERING FOR THE FLOOR OF THE AREA

For the "area" or "flight" I give the preference to very light – light in both colour and substance – porous sand. This should be placed several inches thick on the top of a bedwork of coarse material, such as bricks, and other builders' refuse, large cinders, or other substances that will quickly absorb the surface moisture.

OUTFIT FOR CLEANING THE PIGEON HOUSE

The implements for cleaning the pigeon–house are few and simple, the one of most importance being a sharp steel or iron scraper, to which should be attached a short wooden handle . A common garden rake, with rather closely set teeth, is also necessary, with which to gather up the manure from the floor of the house, and to be used daily in freshening up the sand or gravel in the area or flight.

A plastic bucket should also be provided to remove the refuse. Add to these a good hard broom or sweeping–brush, and an ordinary hand brush, and you have all the outfit necessary to perform the various cleansing operations which should be conducted daily, cleanliness in pigeon keeping being one of the secrets of success.

A little practice will enable a handy man to quickly clean up a long range of houses. A well-kept pigeonry not only enhances the pleasure of viewing and studying the birds, but even the birds themselves revel in freshly cleansed apartments.

VERMIN

Whatever the style or extent of the pigeonry, means must be taken to exclude cats, rats, mice and sparrows. Rats as well as cats are particularly fond of pigeon flesh, and soon make sad havoc in a loft of valuable birds. Therefore, the fancier must pay particular attention to the means of "in" and "out" of his pigeon-house. Cunning as they are, cats may be kept "at bay" with greater ease than can those wretched marauders – rats. Once they obtain the mastery it is difficult to exterminate them; watch should, therefore, be kept for the first sign of the approach of Mr. Rat, and steps promptly taken to effectually put an end to his existence before he has had time to gain admittance to the sacred precints of the pigeonry.

RATS (AND MICE) AND HOW TO DESTROY THEM

At one time the ratcatcher was an essential requirement , but these days the *Warfarin* type of bait, hidden away from all other livestock, can quickly destroy any rats. Put in a porch or other spot not accessible to the birds the bait will soon be eaten and then dead rats will appear. Try to incinerate the bodies to avoid contamination or the poisoning of innocent animals.

CHAPTER 6
MANAGEMENT IN THE BREEDING SEASON

SETTING A TIMETABLE

The most interesting period of the year is that which is usually designated the "breeding season", a term that certainly admits of great elasticity in the minds of many breeders, and may extend from early in the new year until quite late in autumn. Whilst granting that it is fully in accord with the laws of human nature that the breeder of high–class pigeons should wish to obtain as many youngsters as possible (especially if they happen to be of the sort that is wanted), it is highly desirable, not only in the interests of the "fancy", but also for the well being of the parent birds, that some limit should be placed upon this "close season".

It was a custom with the fanciers of bygone days to inaugurate their columbarian marriages for the season on or about St. Valentine's day (14th February), and this is a very good rule to follow. It must be borne in mind that great injury *may* be done by "pairing up" too soon. No hard–and–fast rule can, however, be laid down that would be applicable to all varieties. It therefore becomes necessary to make a careful survey of the leading properties of each – not forgetting their stamina and constitution – before deciding what is (or should be) their most suitable breeding season.

THE TIMES FOR MATCHING

The time for matching depends on the type of pigeon.To more clearly convey my ideas, I propose to divide the different varieties into sections thus:

Section I – Carriers, Dragons, Barbs and Antwerps.
Section II – Pouters, Jacobins and Trumpeters.
Section III –English Owls, Turbits, Eastern Frills,

Fantails, Nuns, Magpies, Longfaced Tumblers, Pigmy Pouters, Show Homers, etc.

Section IV – Shortfaced Tumblers and Foreign Owls.

Under Section I, are classed the varieties in which *an abnormal development of wattle* plays an important part in their chief characteristics, and so much so that to breed these varieties with success and credit to their owners, it is necessary to make an early start in the season, especially if it is desired to take part in the early competitions for young birds.However, it should be noted that highly meritorious youngsters can be bred much later in the season than the months in which the early ones are produced – indeed, it will be found that the winning youngsters at the big autumn and winter exhibitions are rarely traceable to the early nests.

Varieties enumerated under Section I, may be matched up soon after the New Year begins, and although the temperature of the early days of January is rarely of that genial character so necessary for the quick development of newly–hatched squabs, it is none too soon to commence pairing up "on paper", to be followed by the various processes that usually ensue, so that even a "start in the breeding line" thus early will not be productive of many youngsters before the middle or end of February, when the days commence to perceptibly lengthen, and we may, not unreasonably, begin to hope for the pigeon's delight – "just a little sunshine".

I have invariably found that the young of the wattled varieties of pigeons cease to show that much–desired quality if hatched after the month of July. I would therefore say; discontinue breeding these varieties as soon after the end of June as possible.

Section II

Pouters, Jacobins and Trumpeters being all long feathered

birds shall be honoured with a division (II) all their own. The "pairing up" of these varieties should, in my opinion, take place as early as possible after the middle of January, if their leading characteristics are to be reproduced and maintained, as it is rarely that long–feathered youngsters are produced late in the year. Therefore the breeding season of these varieties should be a short and sharp one, i.e. short in duration and sharp in the development of that length of feather so much prized by the fancier of either the Pouter, the Jacobin, or the Trumpeter.

Section III (including Fantails)

Section III comprises a long list of varieties that are neither long–feathered nor heavily wattled, so that in matching up any of these a greater latitude may be allowed, and the breeder cannot go far wrong if he allow the breeding to extend from the **beginning *to the end* of February**, in which case March, with its searching and killing east winds, will be pretty well advanced before the earliest of youngsters make their appearance.

These and subsequent "nests" will have ample time before the real show season commences to develop all those valuable properties for which the enthusiastic fancier fervently hopes. I would just add that the varieties enumerated in this section *may be* successfully bred until quite late in autumn, though it is not, in my opinion, advisable to let them go to nest again after the middle of August.

Section IV (Late Breeders)

Experience of many years teaches me that we pay the penalty of undue haste in the matching up of such small and comparatively delicate varieties as the Short–faced Tumbler and African Owl, not only in the loss of many an old bird, but also in the rickety offspring of these varieties, so that unless the loft is exceptionally favourably situated **do not commence breeding operations with either of these varieties until March is well on the wane**; and do not overbreed.

Note: These are the general rules, but remember that the age of the birds , the location and many other factors must be considered. I have had *very early* birds breed successfully and yet a **tried pair,** mated up in July, the hen died with egg binding in a thunder storm. She was a small , beautifully–shaped fantail , but a large egg , high temperature and possibly fright killed her whilst she tried to lay the second egg of the clutch. It was very sad.

CLEANING THE PIGEON HOUSE

An annual cleaning and decorating is essential. Firstly, then, remove all perches (which should be movable), food utensils, and other appliances; then proceed to scrape off as much as possible of the accumulated dirt and limewash . Then scrub and scour with warm water and household cleaner such as *Flash*. The house should then be allowed to dry before proceeding to apply the very essential coat of limewash or Emulsion paint.

The **old fashioned method** was to use limewash for decorating and disinfecting. Modern emulsion paints have replaced this method, but lime does control insect life and for those who wish to be 'old fashioned' a formula is given below.

THE BEST LIME–WASH

The procedure is as follows: A month or so beforehand procure a few lumps of unslaked lime; place this in a larger bucket or container than may seem necessary; by the addition of *just sufficient* water to induce the lime to "fall", the process of "hydrating" or "slacking" takes place. On the following day more water should be added, so as to form a sort of stiff putty, with just a little excess of moisture. In a few weeks, it will assume the appearance and consistency of a creamy–white emulsion paste, which is the foundation with which to prepare a wash that can be relied upon to make snowy white the living area for the fantails.

Place in an ordinary-sized pail or bucket about 4lb. weight of the lime putty (the manufacture of which I have just described)and add liquid soap, to make the brush work freely; add gradually sufficient water, stirring until the mixture assumes the consistency of new milk. Now add as much powdered alum as will cover the palm of the hand, to make the wash adhere to the wood and brickwork,and not your clothes every time you enter the loft. Lastly, add about a teaspoonful of strong disinfectant, to act as a warning to those little "varmints" commonly called fleas, etc., that their presence is not required in the pigeon house.

A couple of coats of this wash, preceded by the thorough cleansing as indicated, will speedily transform the dullest and dirtiest apartment into a veritable model abode for fantails.

HOW TO PAIR THE BIRDS

We now pass on to that most interesting part of pigeon culture, the actual matching and pairing of the birds, a time that is full of deep import in the mind of the true fancier, for much of his future success or chagrin depends upon the skill he displays in "putting the birds together".

A pairing cage must be provided. This may either be specially constructed, or the ordinary wire pens as used at Shows – of which every fancier should possess a few – may be requisitioned for the purpose, indeed, where a large number of birds have to be paired the wire pens will be found the more convenient arrangement. We will suppose the fancier already has them at hand, fitted up in his food store or pen room. It is therefore simply necessary to divide them into sections by covering up with cardboard the division between every other compartment. With a minimum of trouble you have thus a number of matching pens ready at a moment's notice to receive the various pairs of birds it has been decided to "put together" for the season's breeding.

Figure 6.2   Pairing Cages
Get the birds used to each other ready for pairing.

Another advantage of transforming the wire pens of the show room into temporary "wooing" quarters, is that a number of pen Birds may be caged simultaneously, and thereby facilitate the preliminary studying and selecting of the specimens it is intended to breed from. Having chosen the birds, they should be placed in adjoining pens. If they are in a sound healthy condition, the mating process will quickly begin.In the course of two or three days the birds may be allowed to occupy the same pen, though it is inadvisable to *leave them* together until you are quite sure they are properly paired, for it sometimes happens that the hen refuses to listen to the voice of the cock and rejects him. It is therefore essential to closely watch the movements of the birds before finally putting them together.

Having effectually paired the birds they may be turned into the loft or house that has *previously been prepared for their occupation*, and if possible all the birds that are to occupy one compartment should be put down simultaneously. There may be a few slight differences to "settle" at the outset, as it is very likely that more than one pair of birds will desire to take possession of a favoured corner, but the strife will only be of short duration, and it will be found that in less than twenty–four hours each pair of birds will have secured suitable quarters, which they may be trusted to retain.

BREEDING BOXES

Having cleansed the house and paired the birds it becomes necessary to prepare for their reception by providing the necessary breeding requisites. Firstly, then, I cannot too strongly recommend the use of *moveable* nest boxes; the advantages are so many and the disadvantages so few – practically *nil* – that I will not unnecessarily lengthen this chapter by going too deeply into the why and wherefore, though I may briefly state that for the convenience of cleaning operations alone the moveable nest box possesses many advantages. The sketches illustrate the kind of box that I have used with much success. As regards their durability, I may just remark in passing that I have at present in use a number of boxes that have been constantly "on the go" for a number of years, and they are still for all practical purposes "as good as new".

The dimensions of these boxes may vary somewhat according to the variety kept, but for most breeds the following will be found a useful size: Length 24 in.; width 12 in.; height at back 22 in.; height in front 16 in.; (7 in. below landing board and 9 in. above). The side screens are optional.

The lid should comprise about three–quarters of the entire roof, and should be hung with **T** hinges, as shown in the sketch, as as to open freely, and t.,us facilitate an inspection of the nest, and the necessary cleaning operations. The most suitable material to use in the construction of these boxes is $5/_8$ in. board, using $3/_4$ in. stuff for the bottom. Reference to the sketch shows a

Figure 6.3 Breeding Box

Hinged lid allows inspection of nest

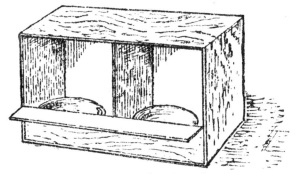

Figure 6.4 An Alternative Breeding Box

Suitable for fantails -- they live in harmony.

Figure 6.5 A double--tier Breeding Box

division between each nest, on the top of which should be nailed a strip of wood about $2^1/_2$ in. wide, inside the box, extending to a landing board, about 5 in. by 4 in. outside, the corners of which should be nicely rounded off, to prevent injury to the birds when suddenly entering or leaving the box.

It will, perhaps, be as well to explain that the box is "roofed" to prevent the top being used as a platform for discouraging those *quarrelsome* customers present in most lofts, and in which the propensity to fight is unduly developed. I must also point out that the height from A to D is fixed at 7 in., so as to keep the youngsters within bounds until they are able to forage for themselves.

By adopting this "moveable dwellings act" each pair of birds can be accommodated with a house all to themselves, and it can moreover be placed exactly in position as *they* prefer, which, as most experienced breeders can testify, will not in all probability be in the most approved methodical or geometrical line, for pigeons, like men, have whims and fancies of their own, which they must to a certain extent be allowed to carry out if peace and goodwill are to reign supreme.

Chief amongst the advantages of this box arrangement are:

1.   The sitting bird is *sufficiently* screened from the others, and without the exclusion of that light and warmth so necessary in the successful rearing of vigorous youngsters.

2.   The youngsters are kept nice and snug in "bed" until they have gained strength enough to hop over the barrier, when they should be able successfully to beat a hasty retreat in the event of a cruel attack from a neighbouring couple.

3.   The youngsters receive better attention from the parent birds when the breeding arrangements of *each pair* are confined to one box, than when the preliminaries for a second nest are going forward in some other quarter of the loft.

Examples of boxes used on a regular basis are given on the preceding page; they can be made quite easily and modified as necessary.

Another type of box , which may be supplied in duplicate, are preferable to the "two-deckers", but are by no means suitable for all varieties. Many years' experience prompts me to strongly impress upon my readers the desirability of placing *all* breeding boxes upon the floor of the loft, i.e. if they wish to avoid frequent mishaps, and consequent vexation. There are not, I am afraid, many fanciers who cannot point with regret to the loss of many a promising youngster as the result of a fall from its nest, where the "nursery" has been injudiciously placed "up aloft".

NEST PANS

Having dealt exhaustively with breeding boxes, nest-pans next claim our attention, and although I am aware that my views will not be shared by everyone, I must again challenge my experience, for it teaches me that the most suitable material for the manufacture of the nest pan for pigeons is that which is commonly called "earthenware". Having *tried* the much-vaunted wooden bowls, I can candidly say that I do not like them, and for very valid reasons: because wood is not a retainer of heat; because these bowls soon become impregnated with ammonia, and other offensive matter; and because they can neither be so readily nor so effectually cleansed as the earthenware pans.

Figure 6.6 Nest Pan indicating the ideal shape

Besides which, the earthenware pan *is* really a good *retainer* of heat, and this is a matter of much importance, more especially during the cold and chilly early months of the breeding season. I have therefore no hesitation in strongly urging breeders of pigeons to use earthenware nest–pans to the exclusion of all others, the sketch (fig. 6.6), showing the shape of the "pan".

The pigeon cannot by any stretch of the imagination be considered an indolent bird, yet it is necessary that the "nest" should be *partly* prepared, and this is best done by placing a few handfuls of "spent" sawdust in each pan. I advocate the use of "spent" sawdust in preference to that which is fresh from the mill, for the simple reason that the shell of the egg being of an absortent nature, the contents are liable to be affected by the absorption of the volatile turpentine that is contained in newly–made pine and deal sawdust. The birds should be allowed to add a few twigs of soft heather, or straw, in accordance with their own views of the situation. If the material is cut up into lengths of about five or six inches, and strewed about the floor of the pigeon house, the carrying of it to the nest, bit by bit, will be a congenial employment for the newly–married couple. Not only this, but in the case of a "fast–driving" cock, this having something else to do will frequently relieve the hen from *too much* attention, andresultant premature laying.

The excrement from a pair of half–grown and thriving squabs will soon transform a breeding–box into a veritable quagmire, unless some absorbent be placed around the pan, and for this purpose nothing can possibly beat a good layer of *fresh* pine sawdust or a thickness of peat moss litter, either of which, being easily removed and renewed, the whole "arrangement" is kept in a clean, sweet, and sanitary condition.

A CONVENIENT STUD REGISTER

A register is most desirable, and a simple yet effectual way of recording the "doings" of each pair is to nail up a card (similar to sketch) over each breeding box, and upon which should be written a description of the stud birds, as well as the breeding number of each pair, date of laying, number of young hatched, when rung (with NPA ring), and when marked off with a corre-sponding number to that of the parent pair. Any note concerning either may be made out at the foot of each card.

These, then, are all the notes at present necessary, and from which later on may be prepared the most complete stud-book.

To avoid errors, the "numbering" should take place before the youngsters leave the nest, as it is sometimes difficult to recognise them when once on the wing, especially in lofts in which a number of birds of the same colour and variety are bred.

BREEDING STUD RECORD CARD

Pair No. 1

Year:19..   Cock.   Cup
              Hen.   1st.

Laid	Young	Rung	Numbered
Feb. 15	1	X	X
March 17	2	X	
April			
May			
June			

N.B. – Above hen is liable to be egg-bound

RINGING

The institution of rings for recording the ages of pigeons, and thereby safeguarding genuine youngsters in the show pen, must be voted the greatest boon of our time. Rings may be obtained from the National Pigeon Association.

These rings should be put on when the youngsters are from eight to ten days old. At that age they can be easily slipped over the feet, and there is little or no risk of their falling off, as is frequently the case when put on *too soon*.

A MOST IMPORTANT POINT

Constant supervision of the birds is very necessary if accidents and mishaps are to be effectually guarded against. Whilst advocating that the breeding birds should be permitted to enjoy as little disturbance as possible, it must not be forgotten that a certain amount of supervision is absolutely necessary; for instance:

1. A pair of birds may suddenly (especially at the commencement of the breeding season) take it into their heads to separate , in which case they speedily form fresh attachments, and thus disorganise the whole colony; or

2. a hen may be egg-bound, and need prompt attention if her life is to be spared; or

3. the squabs may be imperfectly fed, and need artificial assistance; or

4. the stronger of a pair of youngsters may be greedily receiving all the food from the parent birds, whilst its nest mate is actually starving for a portion of that supply of nourishment which, according to the "laws of pigeonry", should be equally divided between the two.

These, then, and many other important considerations, demand one's close and regular attention, if success is to crown our efforts of the season.

THE NECESSITY FOR GRIT

It is essential to provide a mixture, especially during the breeding season, when the strain upon the old birds is great, and the youngsters are in process of development and growth.Flint grit for digestion -- used in the gizzard-- and calcium for shells and body needs are both essential, at the size appropriate for the fantail. Poultry grit tends to be too large.

REMOVAL OF YOUNGSTERS

An important detail in connection with the successful rearing of pigeons is that the youngsters should, in due course, be removed from the breeding loft, and placed in a compartment by themselves. The proper time to make this shift being is when the youngsters "take to the wing" or simultaneously with the entry into existence of the succeeding nest of squabs. Such a "nursery house" is most useful. In it "the babes" are safe from cruel attacks, frequently made by the old birds when engaged in feeding younger offspring.

Another advantage is that a little special attention can be given to the removed youngsters. They can thus be "pushed ahead" by the timely and discriminate use of "extra feeding" which they would not be permitted to indulge in if left to forage for themselves among older and more vigorous birds.

OVERCROWDING

I cannot too strongly caution the inexperienced breeder against the all too prevalent system of overcrowding the stud birds. Three or four pairs of *most* varieties are as many as should be allowed to occupy one compartment. I would, however, make exception in the case of some of the docile breeds such as fantails, by allowing, say, 6 pairs to "go together". It will be found that the percentage of youngsters will be all the greater by taking this advice and allowing the breeding birds ample space.

CHAPTER 7

FEEDERS

'WET NURSING'

Many varieties of "fancy" pigeons may be trusted to rear their own young, but the breeders of Carriers, Pouters, Short-faced Tumblers, Barbs, Turbits, Owls, Trumpeters and **Fantails early in the season** will need a supply of "feeders", or foster parents, if youngsters are to be reared. Although birds of *each* of these varieties are to be occasionally met with that are fairly good nurses, it will, as a rule, be found that they are either too indolent or *unable* sufficiently to feed their offspring.

The "feeders" may be either cross-bred or pure, provided they are by nature tame and domesticated, and will not readily resent the very needful interference of the owner. Common Antwerps, or *half-bred* Pouters, or Croppers, are admirably adapted for rearing the young of Carriers and Pouters, but for the smaller varieties, "feeders" of similar size should as far as practicable be provided, thus: Flying Tumblers, Magpies or Homers, or crosses of any of these may be depended upon to love, cherish and rear the squabs of non-reliable parents.

Feeders should **not** be relegated to a cramped, crowded, and ill-ventilated loft, but must be well housed and well fed, if they are to successfully carry out their maternal duties. If possible, these "foster parents" should have entire liberty, suitable accommodation for which is described in the chapter on loft construction. An arrangement of this kind tends largely to the health and vigour of both "feeders and fed".

PIGEON MILK

Before proceeding further it will be well to point out that the supposed mythological "Pigeon's-milk" is no myth at all, but is a natural secretion for the sustenance of the newly-hatched "squabs". As the squabs increase in size and strength, the supply of "soft food" (as it is called) is gradually diminished, and as gradually intermixed with *partly softened* grain, until such time as the youngsters are strong enough to receive and digest *hard food,* by which time they soon learn to "forage" for themselves. Pigeon milk is high in protein (17.50%) and is 70% water.

THE UTILITY OF FEEDERS

A few moments' reflection should convince the most casual observer that the unwritten laws of Pigeonry cannot be lightly disregarded.

If "feeders" happen to lay simultaneously with the stud birds, it is a good plan at once to transfer their eggs to the nest of the "breeders", and *vice –versa,* but it must be carefully noted that unless an arrangement of this kind can be *assured* it will be safer to wait until the squabs are "out"; they may then be either left with the parent birds for a few days to "feed off" the soft food, or at once exchanged with the offspring of the nurses. To ensure an ample supply of suitable nourishment care must be taken that the ages of these transferred infants are nearly identical.

An exception to this rule may *sometimes* be made with advantage, thus: If the pedigree squabs happen to hatch out a day or two in advance of the young of the feeders, an arrangement of this kind works well – the pedigree youngsters getting an in– creased supply of *soft* food when transferred to their foster parents, while the strain on the stud birds is lessened, the smaller young *from* the feeders being more readily satisfied.

It may be asked, Why should not the stud birds be alto– gether relieved from maternal duties? The answer is plain and simple. Because nature provides them (both cock and hen) with secreted food for the sustenance of their offspring that must be "fed off" if sickness and disorder are to be avoided. It takes from seven to ten days to relieve the crops of the parent birds.

THE REMOVAL OF THE FIRST EGG, ETC.

Some experts in pigeon management recommend the removal of the first egg and the substitution of a dummy, until the second is laid (the object being to ensure the "hatching out" of each simultaneously), but my experience teaches me that this is altogether unnecessary. It will be observed that a pigeon usually stands over – not sits on – its first egg. The process of incubation does not therefore commence until the second egg is laid. *Eighteen days* is the duration of this process, but to simplify calculations it is better to reckon twenty days from the laying of the first egg.

A newly–hatched pigeon is a most helpless creature. For the first few hours of its existence it is sustained by warmth alone – indeed, so important is *natural* warmth in the rearing of vigorous well developed youngsters that I regard it as essential as suitable food. By natural warmth I mean the heat derivable from the parent birds in the natural process of "brooding".

Quite young pigeons are featherless, and, unlike chickens, can neither feed themselves nor take exercise. But if sound, healthy and well nourished they will grow apace; "something is wrong" if you cannot almost see them grow. It is most interesting to note the rapidity with which young pigeons increase in size.

The *average* weight of a youngster just emerging from eggdom is rather under than over $\frac{1}{2}$ oz.; in the course of two days a healthy and thriving squab will weigh about $1 \frac{1}{4}$ oz.; in four days about 3 oz.; in six days about 5 oz., and at twelve days old about 9 oz. It is quite possible for a young bird in less than a month from its birth to outweigh its parent.

CHAPTER 8
THE MOULTING OF PIGEONS

AN ANNUAL NECESSITY

This is a natural function, and one that is needful to maintain the health, comfort, and well-being of birds of all kinds. The laws of animal economy demand a "change of covering" previous to the advent of the cold season of the year the body, and thus repel the chilling and killing influences of damp and cold.

ADULT BIRDS

A careful observer of nature will notice that as the year advances the feathers of a pigeon become hard and dry, clearly proving that the plumage has done its duty.

Moulting is usually effected without difficulty or great loss of vital force, and if "all is well" this shedding of feathers will commence quite early in summer with the inner flights, followed in July by the "casting" of a few of the head and body feathers, but it is not until about the middle of August that the general disruption takes place. The process of moult then begins in earnest, and should continue without intermission to the end of September or beginning of October.

Whilst granting that a fairly quick moult is desirable, it will be well to point out that it is quite possible for a pigeon to go through the process *too* rapidly, confirmation of this statement being traceable in the case of the common Blue Rock -- a pigeon that exists in a half wild state, moults most gradually (it being rarely seen in a state of semi-nakedness), so that nature here again asserts herself as a reliable guide in this, as in other columbarian matters.

If a pigeon moults too quickly this is a sign of poor management.

YOUNGSTERS

These commence to throw off and replace their "nestling flights" almost as soon as ᵋy leave the nest, but the general moult does not commence until the youngsters are about eight weeks old, and this continues without intermission for several months.

It should be observed that the age of a young pigeon may be pretty well gauged by an examination of its flights, thus:-

If only one "nestling feather" remains, the bird will (speaking broadly) be about six months old; if there are two of these feathers to throw, then the bird will probably be about five months old, and so on.

Sometimes birds are most difficult to moult. The flights and tail feathers may grow to full length sheathed in a skin-like covering, that must be skilfully removed if it does not show signs of breaking away naturally. A word of caution to the novice will not be out of place, and it is this:- Do *not* attempt to relieve the new feather from its "casing" whilst it is in a soft and flexible state.

GENERAL MANAGEMENT DURING MOULT

Warmth and dryness are essential to a *healthy moult.* . This cannot, therefore, be attained if the process is hindered or delayed until the damp, dark, and chilly days of October and November. I would here point out that I do not recommend a **too free use** of the bath at the commencement of the moulting season; once or twice a week, according to the state of the weather, will be ample

A small quantity of hemp or linseed may also be given. Cod-liver oil is also a useful remedy. An occasional dose of cooling medicine, followed by a suitable tonic may in some cases be given with the most beneficial results.A change of diet may also be tried. Also give grit and soluble vitamins ,eg; *Abidec.*

79

Index

80